Extremely WEIRD

ANIMAL DISGUISES

Text by Sarah Lovett

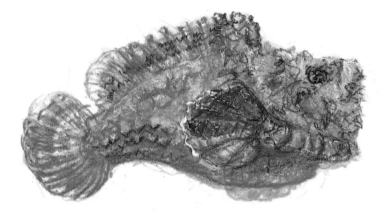

John Muir Publications
Santa Fe, New Mexico

John Muir Publications, P.O. Box 613, Santa Fe, New Mexico 87504

First edition. First printing March 1997.

Library of Congress Cataloging-in-Publication Data
Lovett, Sarah, 1953–
    Animal disguises / text by Sarah Lovett.
        p.   cm. — (Extremely weird)
    Includes index.
    Summary: Describes the physical characteristics and behavior of
such unusually disguised animals as the Malayan leaf insect, the
stonefish, the Brazilian rainbow boa, and the Honduran white bat.
    ISBN 1-56261-357-x
    1. Camouflage (Biology)—Juvenile literature. [1. Camouflage
(Biology)] I. Title. II. Series: Lovett, Sarah, 1953– Extremely
weird.
QL737.L72 1997
591.47'2—dc21   96-49546
                               CIP
                               AC

Extremely Weird Logo Art: Peter Aschwanden
Illustrations: Mary Sundstrom, Sally Blakemore
Design: Sally Blakemore
Typography: Copygraphics, Inc., Santa Fe, New Mexico
Printer: Burton & Mayer, Inc.

Distributed to the book trade by
Publishers Group West
Emeryville, California

Cover photo: Leafy seadragon, courtesy Animals Animals/Oxford Scientific Films © Rudie Kuiter

INTRODUCTION

E very time we step outside we enter a world of natural disguises. Disguises allow animals to look like objects or creatures they are not. What looks like a twig might actually be a stick-like insect. A leaf might be a lizard. If you're in the ocean, you might find stealthy seadragons swimming in the seaweed. And watch where you walk—that rock underfoot might be a fish!

One way animals disguise themselves is through camouflage. Camouflage allows animals to blend in with their surroundings so that it's hard to tell things apart. When animals are camouflaged, other animals, including people, can't see them. Animals also disguise themselves with bright colors. Bright colors usually mean an animal is poisonous, and that's just what harmless animals want dangerous predators to believe. But animals aren't always hiding or playing tricks because they are afraid. Although disguises are commonly used for defense, they are also used for hunting. Predators hide so other animals will come near. The stonefish, like a rock on the seafloor, sits perfectly still and silent while smaller fish swim by unsuspectingly. When meal time comes, the stonefish unveils its mask and surprises its victim.

Animals aren't the only ones in disguise. People use disguises, too. Hunters use camouflage to look like trees in the woods or grass in a field. Make-up is a disguise—people change their faces to look different than they really are. During Halloween, trick-or-treaters disguise themselves to look like monsters, superheroes, and sometimes even animals.

Next time you're outside, look closely at what's around you. You never know what you might find. But before you venture into the wild, see if you can find the animals hidden above. Turn to the glossarized index at the back of this book if you're looking for a specific animal or special information, or if you find a word you don't understand.

GIANT AUSTRALIAN STICK (*Extatosoma tiaratum*)

Walkingsticks and leaf insects all belong to the same scientific family: Phasmidae. As a group, they live mostly in the tropical areas of Asia, although some species have been seen as far north as Europe and North America. Members of this family come in a variety of shapes and colors, and they may resemble green, brown, or rotting leaves, thorns, grass, broken sticks, or stout twigs. One thing they all have in common is camouflage.

Many animals depend on a disguise—protective coloring or shape—to blend in with their background and to hide from predators. Camouflage is especially important for those animals that are not swift in the air or on the ground (a must for quick getaways) or who can't depend on other equipment—poison or armor, for instance—to keep danger away.

During the day, most stick and leaf insects stay almost completely motionless—in strange postures—made invisible by their resemblance to the plants and trees around them. Only the most alert bird or lizard can detect them in the stillness of daylight. They are most active under the cover of darkness, which is when they eat, mate, and drop their eggs.

Leaf insects have wings, but many species of stick insects do not. The giant Australian stick insect lives in Australia, of course.

Scent sense. Most insects have a sharp sense of smell. Some secrete smelly substances to ward off predators or attract mates.

Some of the Asian sticks qualify as the longest insects in the world. They reach a total length of more than one foot!

Photo, facing page, courtesy Animals Animals © R. H. Armstrong

ANIMAL DISGUISES

Heads or Tails?

NORTHERN LEAF-TAILED GECKO *(Phylurrus cornutus)*

CHAK

With more than 800 different types of geckos spread far and wide over the warm areas of the Earth, these lizards are worldly creatures. Although some species of geckos are silent, their name comes from the "geck-oh" sound that others make.

The northern leaf-tailed gecko has a tail that looks like a leaf. In fact, its head looks like a leaf, too. Its entire body is designed to act as camouflage so it blends in with the background. That way, snakes, birds, cats, and other predators can't see the lizard for the leaf—hopefully!

Another way the leaf-tailed gecko uses its head to protect itself is by using its thick, stumpy tail. Since both ends of this gecko look alike, a hungry predator can hardly tell if the leaf-tailed gecko is coming or going.

Noisy! Some geckos are commonly named for the noises they make. Geckos use their tongues and mouths to "geck," "toke," and "chak." That's why you'll find geckos named "tokay" and "cheekchak."

FOOD?

Good-luck geckos! Many folks in Asia believe the "geck" of a gecko brings great fortune (and leaves behind fewer cockroaches, too).

Get a good look at a gecko—the holes behind the eyes are ears!

ANIMAL DISGUISES

6

Photo, facing page, courtesy Animals Animals © Klaus Uhlenhut

HONDURAN WHITE BAT *(Ectophylla alba)*

Tiny Honduran white bats boast long white fur coats, bright yellow ears, and a matching nose-horn. These are very unusual bats found only in the Caribbean lowlands of Central America, where they live on a diet of tropical fruit. Honduran white bats often roost in groups of 2 to 15 members. Their favorite spot is inside a Heliconia leaf. There they make a "tent," by biting into the leaf and folding the leaf over itself. Once inside the tent, they are camouflaged from predators by sunlight that shades their fur soft green to match their background.

In the past, bat guano (droppings) was mined from bat caves to be used as crop fertilizer. Now, guano is being studied for other reasons. A single ounce of guano contains billions of microbes—microbes that may hold the secret to detoxifying industrial waste, creating cleaner fuels, and safer pest control. Scientists are researching what role bat guano plays in maintaining the delicate balance of life within a cave environment.

ANIMAL DISGUISES

From the horse's mouth! Ancient legend has it that sea horse and seadragon remains could cure leprosy, infertility, and rabies, but that's just a tall tale.

In many species of fishes, males are in charge of "child care." Male sea catfish carry eggs and fry by mouth, and male pipefish brood eggs.

LEAFY SEADRAGON (*Phyllopteryx eques*)

Is it a vine? A weed? An exotic plant from outer space? Actually, it is an extremely leafy seadragon camouflaged to look like the seaweed, algae, and eel grass common in the Australian coastal waters where it lives.

Like its relative, the sea horse, the male leafy seadragon is the one who cares for the eggs. He doesn't have a pouch (like the male sea horse). Instead, he packs the eggs below his tail where the skin becomes especially spongy. This happens before the male and female seadragons mate. After the female deposits her eggs underneath the male's tail, his skin hardens into a separate pouch for each egg. When the baby seadragons are ready to swim on their own, out they pop!

Like sea horses, leafy seadragons are not swift swimmers. Instead of speed, they depend on camouflage to avoid predators. Seadragons can change their reddish-brown color to match sea plants, and their leafy limbs sway in the ocean like weeds.

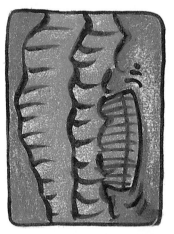

A sea horse uses the feathery fin on its back to travel. This fin vibrates as many as 70 times each second, and each vibration is a complete wave action that ripples top to bottom through the fin. A pair of pectoral fins behind the sea horse's head provides turning and steering power.

Photo, facing page, courtesy Paul A. Zahl/Photo Researchers, Inc.

ANIMAL DISGUISES

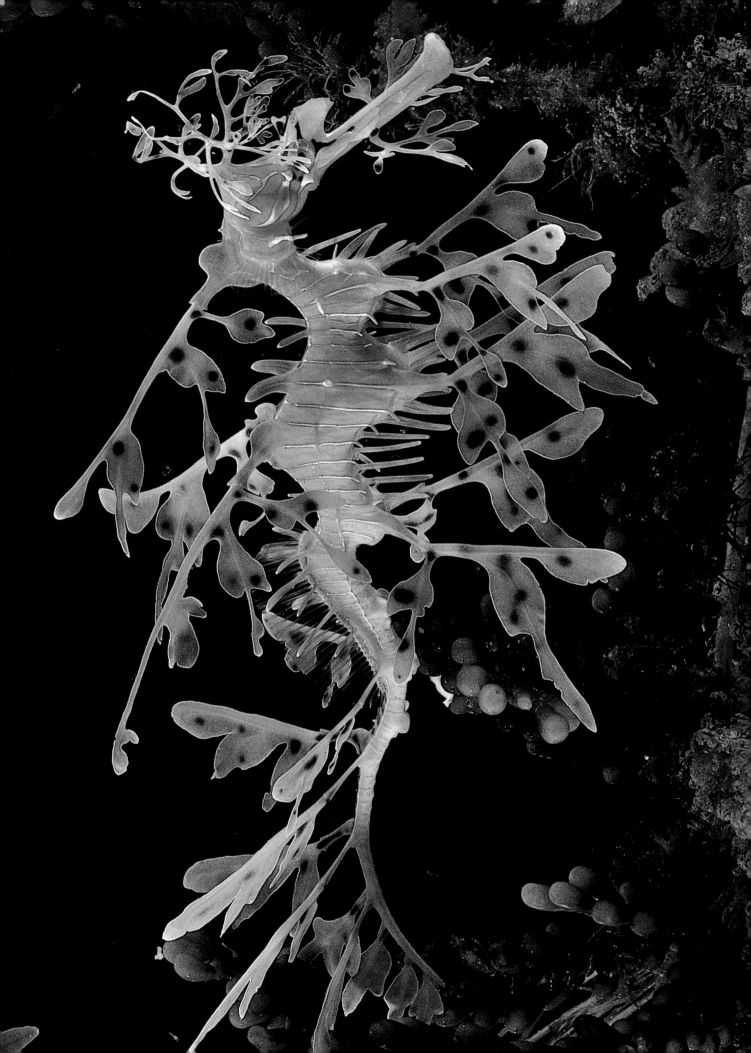

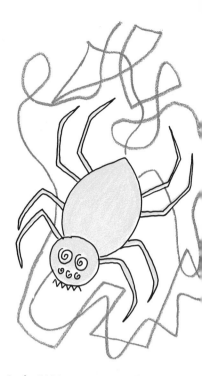

JUMPING SPIDER

Jumping spiders make their living as stalkers and hunters. With their strong eyes and powerful bodies, these brightly colored creatures rule the daylight hours as far as spiders go.

They spot their prey, creep slowly forward, and then pounce! But there are other jumping spiders who have discovered a different way of hunting —and a whole new look.

Ant mimics are jumping spiders, but they look just like ants. They have long and shiny brown bodies, and they even hold their front legs up like antennas and walk on six legs. This "act" allows them to mingle freely with ants. If you're wondering why, it may be because this way they can catch ants very easily. Another reason might be that ants don't taste good and many predators avoid them. Either way, these jumping spiders are great actors.

In the 1960s, scientists studying animal behavior used spiders and their webs for some unusual experiments. When a spider was fed a fly injected with caffeine, it spun a very "nervous" web. When spiders ate flies injected with the hallucinogenic drug, LSD, they spun webs of abstract and wild patterns. But spiders who were given sedatives fell asleep before they finished spinning. The webs were graphic examples of how these drugs affect both spiders and humans.

Recently, NASA launched a spider into orbit to see how its web-building skills worked in zero gravity. It only took the tiny spider three days to learn how to weave near-perfect webs in a weightless environment.

ANIMAL DISGUISES

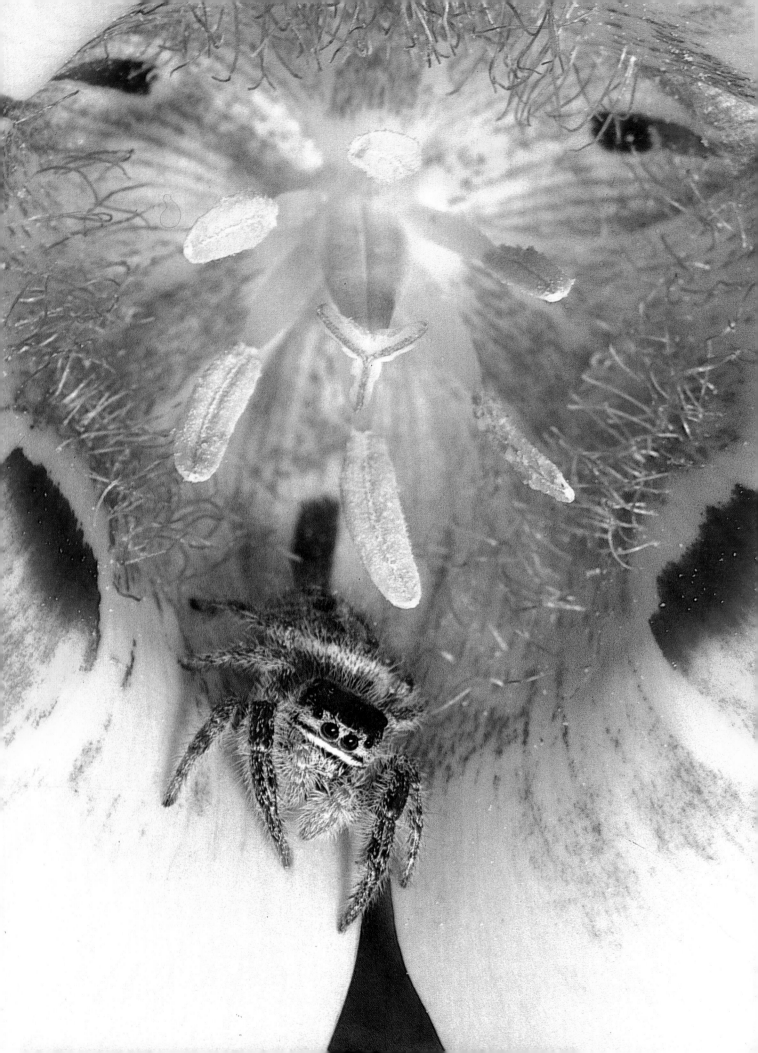

SHORT-HORNED CHAMELEON *(Chamaeleo brevicornis)*

If you keep a quick eye on a slow chameleon, you'll notice some special traits. This animal's swiveling eyes move separately and can look at two things at the same time. (Try moving one of your eyes up and the other sideways and see if you can spot a tiny fly!) And all four of a chameleon's feet look as if they've squeezed into scaly mittens. Chameleon tails are handy (and prehensile!)—these lizards use them to grasp tree branches for balance, for climbing, and just for hanging out.

A chameleon's tongue stays bunched up inside its mouth until it's time to catch a grasshopper or other insect. In action, the tongue shoots out lightning quick and insects stick to the clublike padded tip. Finally, both tongue and insect are reeled back in. That may not seem too weird. After all, you can stick out your tongue and then pull it back in. But imagine if your tongue was as long as your body? And imagine if your aim was so sure that you could ''lick'' an insect on the fly? One thing chameleon tongues *can't* do is stick to damp objects.

Short-horned chameleons from Madagascar are named for the short appendage on their snouts. These critters are especially good at changing colors to match their background, but their change range is only from light yellow to brown. Like many chameleons, they can't turn red or green.

Unlike most lizards, chameleon tails can't be broken off. Chameleons have prehensile tails; they grasp and roll up into perfect spiraling ''seashells.'' Their tails add a special beauty to these little lizards—and also hold onto branches.

Often dull colored, chameleons could be mistaken for tree bark. But true to their names, they do change color. When annoyed, chameleons turn their brightest colors, and so do females about to lay eggs. Chameleons can change shape, too. Flattened, and swaying slowly back and forth, they look like bits of leaves in the wind. These animals are masters of camouflage!

Like all chameleons, the short-horned has cone eyes. Actually, a scale-covered lid surrounds a small opening for the pupil.

Newly hatched or newborn chameleons are on the move and soon! Because they spread out as soon as they can, chameleons don't crowd each other's territory.

DRIVE THRU

BURG

ANIMAL DISGUISES

THE SURINAM TOAD (Pipa pipa)

The South American Surinam toad could easily be mistaken for a flat, square mud pie with two beady eyes. This blackish-brown creature sometimes grows to a length of eight inches and is perfectly camouflaged for the muddy waters of the Amazon and Orinoco rivers where it lives and reproduces.

Surinam toads have a unique way of raising their young. As the female deposits her eggs in water, her mate has a special job to do— he must carefully maneuver 60 to 80 eggs onto the female's back where she will carry them until they hatch.

After the male has completed his task, he retreats, and the female sits quietly for several hours. While she waits, the skin on her back swells up like a sponge and surrounds each egg in a tiny capsule of tissue. Within four months' time, fully formed young toadlets emerge from their mother's back.

All frogs have very sensitive skin, and some even breathe through it. (Of course, frogs also use their lungs to breathe.) Because frogs and other amphibians have such sensitive skin, they are good indicators of environmental conditions. Problems like acid rain, contaminated air and water, and exposure to high levels of ultraviolet sun rays affect frog populations. In fact, concerned scientists are studying a worldwide decline in amphibians.

Photo facing page courtesy Animals Animals © OSF Avril Ramage

ANIMAL DISGUISES

STONEFISH *(Synanceia verrucosa)*

The warty, blobby, blotchy stonefish can be deadly. In fact, it has the most poisonous venom of all fishes! The spines of its dorsal fin (located on its back) are as sharp as hypodermic needles, and they are made for injecting poison. Skin divers must be especially careful because a stonefish is hard to spot. All those warts and blobs on the fish's skin provide camouflage; waiting for unsuspecting prey to swim by, a stonefish looks much like a rock or stone on the ocean bottom. If an unlucky swimmer steps on a stonefish, the pressure of his body weight will cause venom glands (located near the base of the dorsal fin spines) to inject poison into his foot. Stonefish poison has been known to kill a human within two hours of injection!

There are ten species of stonefish; most live in tropical seas where they prefer rocky bottom areas. This particular stonefish lives in Indo-Pacific waters. Some ichthyologists (ick-thee-OL-oh-gists), scientists who study fishes, believe stonefishes are related to scorpionfishes, while other scientists group stonefishes in their very own family: Synanceiidae.

Out of more than 20,000 fish species worldwide, only about 50 are poisonous. Stingrays, stonefishes, and lionfishes are among those that can cause painful problems for humans. But poisonous fishes mostly use their venom as a defense against large fish predators.

Fishy feelies! Landlubbers have nothing to compare with a fish's lateral line. These sensory receptors lining the body of many fishes detect any change in surrounding water pressure, direction, or flow, as well as low-frequency sound.

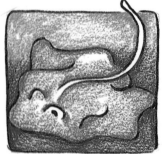

Stingrays—named for the poisonous sting of their whip-thin tail—may weigh more than 500 pounds (almost 300 kg) and have a wingspan greater than 10 feet (3 m). These giants hang out on sandy ocean bottoms and cruise in search of crustaceans and fishes to eat.

Photo, facing page, courtesy Steinhart Aquarium/Photo Researchers, Inc.

ANIMAL DISGUISES

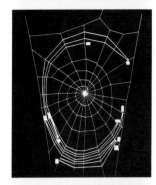

OGRE-FACED STICK SPIDER

With two out of eight eyes like giant head-lamps, stiltlike legs, a humped body that could pass for a thorn, a twig, or a bud, and an odd head, the ogre-faced stick spider looks extremely weird. But looks aren't everything, and this spider is famed for casting its silky "net" over flying prey. For this reason, some people call it the net-casting spider.

Ogre-faced stick spiders spend their days pressed flat against the bark of a tree limb with their front legs stretched out and their back legs holding firm around the branch. This strange perch makes it very hard for passing predators to spot them. But after sundown, it's another story.

The ogre-faced spider begins each evening's work by first spinning a small rectangular net about the size of a postage stamp. The spider holds the little net with its four front legs and uses its back legs to hang onto the main web. Hanging downward, ogre-face waits for the right moment to cast itself forward, with its net stretched 5 or 6 times normal size to catch a passing insect. The unfortunate prey is instantly paralyzed with spider venom, then wrapped in silk and eaten. This same method and net are used all night. When the ogre-faced spider is full, or daylight arrives, it neatly rolls its net into a ball and drops it to the ground.

Models showing the process of weaving the web of *Eperia sericata (sclopellaria)* (Neg. No. 37859; Photo R.C. Lenskjold; Courtesy Department Library Services, American Museum of Natural History)

Step into my parlor, said the spider to the fly. Why do bugs fly into spider webs? Maybe they really are invited. Scientists have recently discovered that some spiders decorate their webs with silk strands that reflect ultraviolet light. And, what do you know, webs with ultraviolet strands attract more bugs than webs without. Apparently, for bugs, ultraviolet light is a sign of the clear blue sky.

Photo, facing page, courtesy Animals Animals © OSF

ANIMAL DISGUISES

Bee Wear

BEE BEETLE *(Trichius fasciatus)*

The bee beetle belongs to the scientific family Passalidae, commonly known as the betsy beetles. There are about 500 species, who inhabit mostly tropical areas of Asia and Central America. Only four species of betsy beetles are found in North America.

While most betsy beetles are large and have powerful jaws and a small horn on their head, the bee beetle is among the smallest of this group. It looks a lot like a small bee, which probably helps it discourage hungry predators. Bee beetles aren't the only bee mimics. Many other insects use "bee camouflage" to protect themselves.

Family groups of adult and larval betsy beetles live together in rotting logs, and they have a definite social structure. Even though it is primitive, the social behavior of this insect family is extremely unusual in beetles.

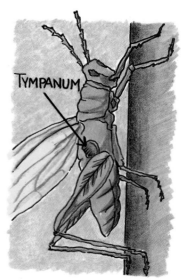

Say what? An extremely delicate built-in drum (tympanum) allows an insect to hear. This membrane is connected to special internal organs; they, in turn, carry impulses to the insect's brain. Depending on the critter, tympana may be located on an insect's antennae, knees, or abdomen.

More than 2,500 years ago, Egyptians tended bees in hives.

Bee scout! Honeybees are social critters. A bee scout who has found nectar will fly back to the hive and tell other bees where to find it. The bee communicates by dancing, and its directions are keyed off the sun. As the day passes, and the sun moves in the sky, the bee adjusts its dance accordingly.

Photo, facing page, courtesy Animals Animals © K. G. Preston-Mafham

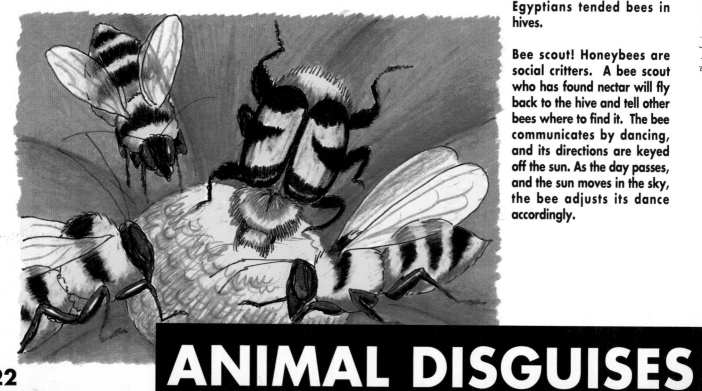

ANIMAL DISGUISES

SPIDER CRAB (Libinia emarginata)

Crabs and lobsters have pinching claws—the better to capture, crush, or rip their prey. These same fierce claws come in handy for defending territory, or for warding off predators.

While crabs wield their claws to escape danger, they also do without them in a pinch. Crabs have breakaway limbs—a special breaking point where the legs attach to the body. When an enemy has a crab by the leg, the leg snaps off, and the crab may escape. There is very little bleeding, and a new limb will grow in stages each time the animal molts its shell (usually once a year).

There are almost 50 spider crab families. Most are bottom dwellers, many are burrowers (who dig in the seabed to escape predators), and some swim using two legs as paddles. Like most members of its family, *Libinia emarginata* covers itself with tiny plants and animals such as sea anemones and sponges for protective camouflage. A well-decorated spider crab is hard to spot!

The world's largest crustacean is the giant spider crab (*Macrocheira kaempferi*), whose name in Japanese means the tall-leg crab. This giant can measure more than 25 feet (8 m) from leg tip to tip! Its claws may be 10 feet (about 3 m) apart when it is ready to attack prey, but its body is only about 18 inches long and 12 inches wide. Giant spider crabs prey on other crustaceans and also echinoderms, worms, and mollusks—never on humans. The largest of these animals may live for twenty years.

Photo, facing page, courtesy Animals Animals © Breck P. Kent

ANIMAL DISGUISES

BRAZILIAN RAINBOW BOA *(Epicrates cenchris)*

Boas are known for their extremely colorful and iridescent skin. This rainbow coloring might seem like the last thing snakes could hide behind, but that's exactly what they do. Orange, yellow, and black patterned Brazilian rainbow boas become almost invisible when sunlight dapples the leaves in their forest habitats in South and Central America. In the right light, you can't see the snakes for the trees.

It is just as difficult to pick out one Brazilian rainbow boa from all the others when they cluster together. Adult boas sometimes form clusters during the mating season. These boas are viviparous, which means they bear live young rather than lay eggs.

Pythons and boas are deaf, but they can "feel" loud noises with their tongues. In fact, a snake's tongue is three sense organs in one: it can touch, smell, and hear.

In cooler northern climates, some garter snakes crowd or coil together in dens to stay warm during winter hibernation. Although the snakes do cool over time, heat loss is reduced.

Photo, facing page, Animals Animals © Paul Freed

ANIMAL DISGUISES

Spiders in Disguise

BIRD-DROPPING SPIDER

Three guesses what the bird-dropping spider looks like! This little crab spider is one of a group that protect themselves by looking like something no one wants to eat. Some are perfect imitations of tiny seeds, leaves, or flowers. But the Malaysian bird-dropping spider has one of the most unusual costumes of all, and it is especially convincing when perched on its web.

For spiders, camouflage works two ways—to discourage predators and to attract prey. When spiders are in disguise, predators like lizards, wasps, and birds may pass them by. But critters that spiders love to eat may think they see a bird dropping when it's really a hungry spider.

Another spider that sometimes imitates a bird dropping is the female bolas spider. This incredible huntress hangs by her back legs from a few strands of silk. With her front legs, she holds a silk line with a sticky blob at the end and waits for a moth to fly by. When her prey is within range, the bolas spider throws her silk line at the moth, "sticks it," and hauls it in to eat.

Australian Aborigines have long used a unique method of fly fishing. Poking the end of a pole into a sticky spider's web, the angler creates a long line of silk. This is dipped into the crushed body of a large silk spider. The rest of the spider's body and the fishing line are tossed into a stream where fish gather. As the fish bite at the scraps, their mouths are tangled in the silk and they are pulled to shore.

Photo, facing page, courtesy Animals Animals © OSF

ANIMAL DISGUISES

Leaf Me Alone

MALAYAN LEAF INSECT *(Phyllium pulchrifolium)*

Huge Malayan leaf insects have wings and legs, and the sides of their body are flat and uneven like the edges of a leaf. To make matters even leafier, they are green, yellow, or brown.

During the day, they hang motionless, almost in a trance. When they do move, it is in slow motion, and they look like leaves blowing gently in the wind. Leaf insects have a special reflex action known as thanatosis, or playing dead. When they are startled, they automatically drop from their perch and stay perfectly still wherever they land.

Female leaf insects are flightless; they have lost their hind wings, although they do have leaflike front wings. Males *do* fly and are usually much smaller than females. The record length of a stick insect is 13 inches, but most are from 1 to 5 inches long.

All stick and leaf insects are herbivores (or plant eaters). Some species may reproduce in such numbers they can strip large areas of woodland. Commonly, they reproduce by parthenogenesis, which means the eggs are not fertilized by the male and develop into more females.

Malayan leaf insects of the genus Phyllium live in Malaysia and other areas of tropical Asia and Indonesia.

Walkingsticks, like leaf insects, depend on camouflage for protection from predators; they mimic the sticks around them. Some walkingsticks can stay still for more than 6 hours at a time!

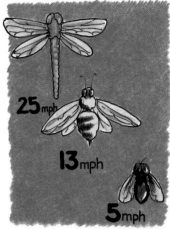

25mph

13mph

5mph

Call me speedy! Hawkmoths and dragonflies are the race cars of insects; they commonly cruise at 25 mph. Honeybees clock in at about 13 mph, butterflies at 12 mph, and house flies reach a slowpoke cruising speed of only 5 mph. And we still can't catch them!

ANIMAL DISGUISES

This glossarized index will help you find specific information on animals and animal disguises. It will also help you understand the meaning of some of the words used in this book.